Master Your Money

Know YOUR MONEY

Izzi Howell

illustrated by Yekyung Kwon

PowerKiDS press

Published in 2026
by The Rosen Publishing Group, Inc.
2544 Clinton Street, Buffalo, NY 14224

First published in Great Britain in 2023 by Hodder & Stoughton
Copyright © Hodder & Stoughton, 2023

Editor: Izzi Howell
Designer: Tim Bond

Cataloging-in-Publication Data
Names: Howell, Izzi, author. | Kwon, Yekyung, illustrator.
Title: Know your money / by Izzi Howell, illustrated by Yekyung Kwon.
Description: Buffalo, NY : PowerKids Press, 2026. | Series: Master your money | Includes glossary and index.
Identifiers: ISBN 9781499453911 (pbk.) | ISBN 9781499453928 (library bound) | ISBN 9781499453935 (ebook)
Subjects: LCSH: Money--Juvenile literature. | Finance, Personal--Juvenile literature.
Classification: LCC HG221.5 H694 2026 | DDC 332.4--dc23

All rights reserved.

No part of this book may be reproduced
in any form without permission in writing from the publisher, except by a reviewer.

Manufactured in the United States of America
CPSIA Compliance Information: Batch #CSPK26. For further information contact Rosen Publishing at 1-800-237-9932.

Find us on

Words in **bold** appear in the glossary on page 30.

CONTENTS

Money, money, money	4
Around the world	6
Digital dollars	8
Cryptocurrencies	10
Making money	12
Bank basics	14
Loans	16
Brainy borrowing	18
Tax	20
Rich ...	22
... and poor	24
A helping hand	26
The future of money	28
Glossary	30
Further information	31
Index	32

MONEY, MONEY, MONEY

Today, people say that money makes the world go round. But money isn't anything new. We've been using it to pay for things for thousands of years!

Starting with shells

The first items used as money were natural objects, such as cowrie shells. Starting around 1200 **BCE**, these shells were used by traders across parts of Africa, Asia, and Europe.

Cash money

The first metal coins were used in the 7th century BCE in what is now Turkey. Over 1,000 years later, the first paper notes, or bills, appeared in China. They were made from the bark of mulberry trees.

I guess money really does grow on trees!

Modern money

Today, metal coins and paper notes are used all over the world. Metal coins are usually round but can be made from different kinds of metal. Some countries have replaced their paper notes with plastic notes, which last longer.

I'm super strong!

MONEY MISSION

What does the money look like in your country? How many different coins do you use? What kind of notes do you have?

AROUND THE WORLD

Most countries have their own type of money. This is known as its **currency**.

Countries and currencies

Which currency do you use in your country? In the UK, they use British pounds. In China, people use the yuan. Some currencies from different countries have the same name. For example, Australia, the United States, and Canada all have a currency called the dollar, but each country's dollar is worth a different amount.

Money mates

A few currencies are used in more than one country. Many of the countries in the European Union (EU), including France, Spain, and Germany, use the euro. This makes it easier for people to travel and trade within the EU.

Making the change

Today, most people use **debit** or credit cards to pay for items abroad. You may also be able to use your card to take out cash in the country's currency. However, you might be charged an extra fee, so be careful!

More or less?

When you **exchange** your currency, you'll receive a different amount of money in the new currency. This is because different currencies are worth different amounts. For example, if you exchanged $1 American into Indian rupees, you'd get just around 86 rupees.

DIGITAL DOLLARS

Today, people are choosing more and more to pay for things **digitally** rather than with cash. Digital money can make life easier, but it does come with problems too.

Cards and more

You can pay for items digitally using a card linked to your bank account (see pages 14–15). You can also link your bank account to other devices, such as your phone, tablet, or smartwatch.

Quick and easy

In the past, the only way to pay by card was by putting it into an **ATM** (automated teller machine) and typing in your secret **PIN**. Today, many places offer **contactless** payments. All you need to do is tap your card, phone, or other device against the card reader and ta-da! You paid!

No cash needed

Many people prefer to pay digitally, as they don't have to remember to carry cash or worry about losing it. Digital payments can also be easier for businesses. A cashless business doesn't have to keep cash in the till for change or go to the bank to put it into their account.

Digital downsides

However, paying digitally comes with risks. If your card or phone gets lost, the money in your account can be stolen. It's also very easy for someone to make contactless payments with your card, as you don't need to know the PIN.

CRYPTOCURRENCIES

Some people think that these virtual currencies are the future of money! But many people don't actually understand what **cryptocurrencies** are and how they work, so here's a quick guide.

Basic bits

Cryptocurrencies are a totally digital form of money. You can't take them out of the bank. They can only be used to pay for things online. The most famous cryptocurrency is Bitcoin, but there are thousands of others.

Making money

Unlike other types of currency, cryptocurrencies can be mined (created by solving very difficult math problems on a computer). However, you need a very, VERY powerful computer to do this! Cryptocurrencies can also be bought using normal money.

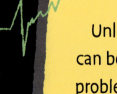

Change to crypto?

Cryptocurrencies can be used anywhere in the world, so you don't have to worry about exchanging money. Recently, some cryptocurrencies have become very valuable, which has made cryptocurrency **investors** very rich.

Crypto concerns

Other people are worried about the risks of cryptocurrencies. Unlike normal money, they aren't controlled by a government, so their **value** goes up and down a lot. It is easy for people to suddenly lose a lot of money. Creating cryptocurrency is also bad for the environment, as the powerful computers require huge amounts of energy.

MAKING MONEY

There are many different ways of **earning** money. The money that we receive is called **income**.

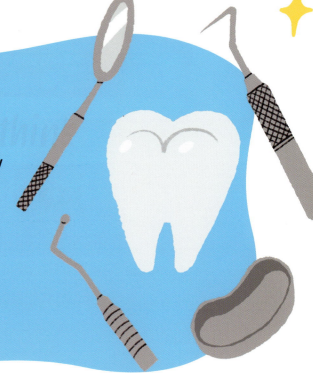

Work, work, work

Most adults work to earn money. The money that they earn is called their **salary**. Some jobs have higher salaries than others. Jobs with higher salaries, such as dentist or lawyer, often require specialized skills and lots of training.

MONEY MISSION

Children can earn money too! Ask your family or close friends if there are any chores you can do for extra money. You could offer to clean, help in the garden, or look after pets. Always check in with your parent or caregiver first.

A helping hand

Some people receive money from the government to help them pay for housing, food, and other everyday needs. It is given to people who are looking for a job, need extra support, or can't work because they have a disability, are ill, or are looking after their children.

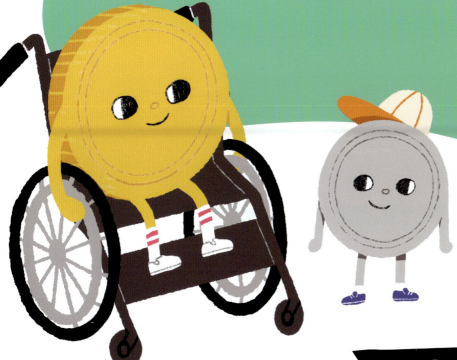

Time to retire

In many countries, people choose to stop working when they are in their sixties. This is called **retirement**. Some retired people may receive a **pension**. Others have saved money in special retirement accounts.

Happy Retirement!

BANK BASICS

Once you have some money, it's important to keep it safe! Cash is easy to spend (and lose), so storing your money in the bank can be a better option. Your money is kept in a bank account.

In the bank

Many banks offer special accounts for young people. First, you'll need some money to get started! You can **deposit** (put) cash into your account at the bank, or you can transfer money from another bank account.

Cool cards

Older teenagers and adults are usually given a card with their account. This card can be used to **withdraw** (take out) money from an ATM or to buy items in stores or online. Cards should be kept in a safe place. Only share your card details with your family.

Keeping track

Be careful! You can only spend the money that you have in your account. Check your account balance regularly.

+5, +10, -2.50, -1.99, -3.75

MONEY MISSION

If you don't have a bank account, keep your cash as safe as possible by placing it in one secure place, such as a piggy bank. When you go shopping, carry your money in a wallet or purse, rather than loose in your pocket or a bag.

LOANS

Have you ever borrowed money from a friend or family member? Adults borrow money too, but usually from the bank. This is called a **loan**. Borrowing money is faster than saving up, but you need to be sure you can afford to pay it back.

Payback

When someone takes out a loan, they usually receive the money right away. Most customers make **repayments** to the bank each month to pay back the loan. They also have to pay the bank extra fees called interest. This is how banks make money.

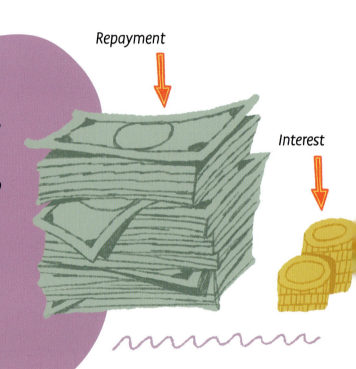

Repayment

Interest

What is debt?

The amount of money that someone owes is known as **debt**. It's normal for adults to have some debt. But too much debt can lead to problems.

Little and big

Some loans are for smaller amounts of money, such as to pay for a new TV. These loans can usually be paid back in a few years. Most people take out a big loan called **mortgage** when they buy a home. They have to make payments to the bank for many years.

On credit

Many adults have a credit card, which is a type of loan. The bank allows you to spend a certain amount of money on your credit card. At the end of the month you have to pay at least some of the money back. If you don't pay it all in time, you may have to pay interest too.

That's enough spending for now!

BRAINY BORROWING

Borrowing money is a big decision! It can be a big help, but it can also have a major effect on your finances. It's important to think through getting a loan carefully before making a decision.

Safe savings

One of the benefits of borrowing money is that you don't have to use up all of your savings to buy something expensive. This leaves you with some money for any unexpected purchases, for example if your phone breaks and needs to be replaced.

Bit by bit

Most bank loans are paid back in monthly repayments. This helps spread out the cost of a big purchase, so you don't have to use up all your money in one go. If you borrow money from a friend or family member, they might let you do this too!

JAN   FEB   MAR

Finance check

Before borrowing money, it's important to look at your finances. How much money do you receive each month from your allowance or extra chores? How much do you normally spend? Do you have enough leftover for monthly repayments? If you can't afford the repayment, you can't afford the loan!

How much?!

Do your research

It's important to borrow money from a safe place, such as a bank. Some companies offer loans that look good at first, but later require very big repayments so people have to pay back much more than they borrowed.

TAX

Most adults have to pay back some of their earnings as **tax**. The government uses tax money to pay for important services and to look after public places.

Taking out tax

In most countries, the amount of tax you have to pay depends on how much money you earn. People who earn more may pay more taxes than those with lower salaries.

Special services

Schools and emergency services, such as the police and the fire department, are paid for with tax money. This means that anyone who needs these services can access them without having to pay anything.

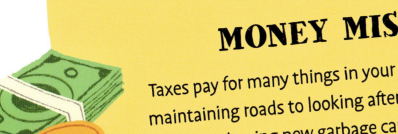

MONEY MISSION

Taxes pay for many things in your neighborhood, from maintaining roads to looking after parks and trees, and sometimes buying new garbage cans! Next time you walk around your neighborhood, take a look and see if you can spot anything else that is paid for with taxes.

Tax trouble

People can have different opinions about taxes. Some think that it's unfair to make people pay for services that they don't use, such as people without children paying for schools. Other people think that we should pay more taxes so that public services are better for everyone. What do you think?

RICH ...

A small number of people around the world are very rich. They live in huge houses, drive expensive cars, and live a life of luxury. The richest of them all are known as the superrich.

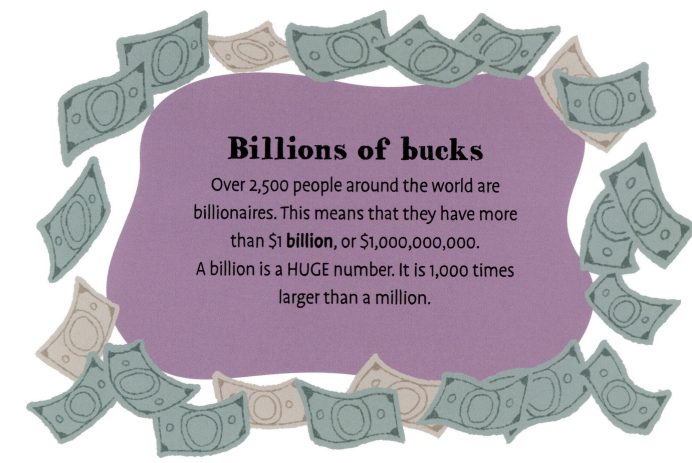

Billions of bucks

Over 2,500 people around the world are billionaires. This means that they have more than $1 **billion**, or $1,000,000,000. A billion is a HUGE number. It is 1,000 times larger than a million.

How to get rich

So how do people become billionaires? Some become rich through hard work, but this is often only part of the story. A few superrich people **inherited** money from their families who built up money over many years. Others were very lucky and started businesses at just the right time.

Mean money

Some billionaires have made their fortunes by treating other people and the planet badly. They pay low wages to the people who work for them, while they make millions. Others have become rich by selling fossil fuels, such as coal, oil, and gas. When these fuels are burned, it leads to **global warming**.

MONEY MISSION

Rich people do work hard, but so do people who earn lower wages. Look at the list of jobs below. Who do you think works hardest? Who do you think deserves to make the most money? Why?

* a garbage collector
* a football player
* a nurse
* a teacher
* a pop star
* an internet influencer
* the owner of an oil company
* a hospital cleaner

... AND POOR

While some people are incredibly rich, many people around the world live in **poverty**. Why is our world so unequal when it comes to money?

Poverty problems

There are lots of reasons why some countries are home to many people living in poverty. Wars and natural disasters—such as earthquakes, droughts and floods, often linked to **climate change**—can force people to leave their homes and jobs, and move to a new area with no way of earning a living.

Unfair finances

Some countries have bad governments that don't share the country's money properly. They might steal tax money instead of using it to help everyone. Foreign companies can take advantage of poor countries. These companies take valuable resources without paying enough money or build factories where local people are paid very low salaries.

Help for others

More economically developed countries often give money to **less economically developed countries**. This money can help to fix simple problems such as buying food for hungry people or rebuilding towns after a natural disaster.

Fair for all

The best way to reduce poverty is by sharing wealth. To do this, people need to pay fair prices for items from less economically developed countries, such as clothing and food.

A HELPING HAND

Poverty affects every country, including more economically developed ones. Here are some ways that you can help out in your community.

Marvelous money

Local charities always welcome cash donations. If you can, why not put aside some of your pocket money to donate to charity? You could donate to the same charity each time, or share your donations across different charities.

Volunteer power

If you don't have money to spare, donate your time instead! Why not offer to organize an event to raise money for the charity, such as a bake sale?

Food for all

Next time your family goes shopping, ask if you can pick up an extra item to donate to your local food bank. Check which items the food bank needs at the moment, so that your donation is useful.

Brilliant banks

Why stop at food? Some communities also have clothes banks and toiletries banks where people can pick up items that they need. Look through your clothes and shelves and see if you have any good-quality clothes or unopened toiletries to donate.

THE FUTURE OF MONEY

From shells and early coins to credit cards and cryptocurrency, money has changed a lot over time. How will it continue to change in the future?

Goodbye to cash!

Nowadays, more and more businesses accept and even prefer for their customers to pay by card. Some people believe that we will eventually become a "cashless society" in which people stop using cash altogether.

Money for everyone

Some countries are considering giving people a universal basic income. This is a regular payment given to all adults. You wouldn't need to work or be looking for a job to receive the money. Supporters think that a universal basic income would reduce poverty. Other people argue that people wouldn't work if they didn't have to. What do you think?

Up and up

The price of most objects generally goes up slowly over time. This is known as inflation. Over the past 30 years, many everyday items, such as bread and milk, have become more expensive because of inflation. In the future, prices will probably continue to rise. People's incomes will need to increase so that they can afford to live well.

Healthy habits

Whatever the future holds, developing good money habits now will help you make the most of your finances later. Use your pocket money to practice skills such as setting money aside as savings, or making a budget. You'll be a pro by the time you earn an income!

GLOSSARY

ATM – a machine from which you can withdraw cash

BCE – before common era, refers to dates before the year 1 CE

billion – one thousand million (1,000,000,000)

climate change – changes to the weather on Earth

contactless – describes a bank card that can pay for something without touching the card machine

cryptocurrency – a type of digital money that isn't controlled by a government

currency – the money that a country uses

debit – having to do with money taken from a bank account to pay for something

debt – the amount of money you need to pay back to a bank or person that you have borrowed money from

deposit – to put in

digital – something online or on a computer

earn – to receive money as payment for a job

exchange – to swap

global warming – the increase in temperatures on Earth mostly caused by human activity

income – money someone earns

inherit – to receive money from someone after they have died

investor – a person who puts money into a business, with the hope of making more money if the business is successful

less economically developed country – a country with a weak economy and low standards of living

loan – money that is borrowed and has to be paid back

more economically developed country – a country with an advanced economy and high standards of living

mortgage – a big loan

pension – money paid to a person, commonly after they have worked for a set time at a company or for the government

PIN – personal identification number, or a code used to access your bank account

poverty – being very poor

repayment – paying something back

retirement – when someone stops working because of their age

salary – the amount of money that someone earns in a year from their job

tax – money from your income paid to the government

value – how much something is worth

withdraw – to take out

Further Information

Books

Be a Young Entrepreneur
by Adam Sutherland and Mike Gordon (Wayland, 2023)

Managing Money
by Nancy Dickmann (Brown Bear Books, 2024)

Websites

natwest.mymoneysense.com/students/students-8-12/how-a-bank-works
Play a game to learn more about how a bank works.

kids.britannica.com/kids/article/money/399548
Learn more about the history of money.

INDEX

bank accounts 8, 9, 14–15

banks 8, 10, 14, 15, 16, 17, 18, 19

billionaires 22

cards 7, 8, 9, 15, 17, 28

charities 26

coins 5

contactless 8, 9

credit cards 7, 17, 28

cryptocurrencies 10–11

currencies 6–7

debt 16

digital money 8–9, 10

food banks 27

governments 11, 13, 20, 24

inflation 29

interest 16, 17

loans 16–17, 18, 19

mortgages 17

pensions 13

PIN 8, 9

poverty 24–25, 26, 28

rich people 22–23

salaries 12, 20, 24

shells 4

taxes 20–21, 24

universal basic income 28